The Time-Value of Money

Jeffrey Pattavina

Leverage Business Group LLC, 2007

2nd Edition, 2026

Contents

1 Introduction 3
   1.1 Time Value of Money 3
   1.2 Market Value 3
   1.3 Book Value 4
   1.4 Intrinsic Value 4
   1.5 Risk-Reward 4
   1.6 Capital 5
   1.7 Cost of Capital 5
   1.8 The capital structure 5
   1.9 WACC: 6
2 Future and Present Value 8
   2.1 *Future Value* 8
   2.2 Future Value of a Cash Flow Stream 10
   2.3 Present Value 11
   2.4 Present Value of a Cash Flow Stream 12
3 Interest 14
   3.1 Simple Interest 14
   3.2 Compound Interest 15
   3.3 Effective Interest 16
4 Annuities 18
   4.1 Annuity 18
   4.2 Present Value of an Annuity 18
   4.3 Future Value of an Annuity 20
   4.4 Payment and Term of an Annuity 22
5 Mortgages 26
   5.1 Mortgages 26
   5.2 Remaining Principal 27
   5.3 Loan, Payments and Periods 28
6 NPV, IRR and MIRR 33
   6.1 Net Present Value (*NPV*) 33
   6.2 Internal Rate of Return (*IRR*) 35
   6.3 Modified Internal Rate of Return (*MIRR*) 38
7 Discounting 43
   7.1 Discount Rate 43
   7.2 Capitalization and Constant Growth 45
   7.3 Two Stage Growth Model 48
8 Appendix 51
9 Bibliography 53

1 *Introduction*

1.1 Time Value of Money

The central idea in *Time-Value Analysis* is to be able to recast the monetary value of one or more future cash flows into an equivalent present monetary value. Converting to *Present Value* allows all future cash flows to be treated within the same time-frame and thereby provides the means necessary to evaluate the asset fairly. Several things affect the *Present Value* of future dollars:

(1) A dollar tomorrow has less purchasing power than a dollar today due to inflation

(2) A dollar today can be invested to grow to a *Future Value* that exceeds its *Present Value*.

The method by which we convert a future cash flow into today's dollars is known as *discounting*. The *Discount Rate* (*DR*) represents the *Cost of Capital* (*COC*), which is the total yield expected from an investment.

1.2 Valuation Types

Assets

An asset is an entity, tangible, or intangible, that holds monetary value. Various standard methodologies are used to determine a fair and reasonable value for an asset.

Market Value

One method for valuing an asset is called market value and is the price as determined in a competitive marketplace. The value is established by comparing the price of similar assets sold with commensurate investment risk.

Book Value

A second method referred to as *book* value, is the price of an asset, less its accumulated depreciation. The *depreciation* of asset is the systematic method for reducing the value of an asset over time.

The book often does not represent the asset's true market value; it represents the asset's equivalent *tax-value*. For example, an investment property can be depreciated to zero over its useful life on the books. However, the asset may still have significant market value.

Book value is typically not used to value assets and most often the book values of assets are recast to *Fair Market Value*.

Intrinsic Value

A third method referred to as *Intrinsic Value* may be thought of as the value based on the future cash flows generated by an asset. The cash flows need to be discounted to *Present Value* using the investor's required *Rate of Return* (*ROR*), also known as *Return on Investment* (*ROI*), or sometimes just *return*. The return on an investment is the (percentage) of money gained or lost relative to the amount of invested.

Risk-Reward

The probability of meeting an expected return is a weighted measure of investment uncertainty or risk. A low probability of achieving the expected returns implies more uncertainty and therefore higher risk.

A high probability of achieving the expected returns implies less uncertainty and therefore lower risk. Typically, higher risk demands higher rates of return. This is a simple risk-reward paradigm.

We will be using the intrinsic value in this paper as a means to value an asset based on the expected cash flows of the asset.

1.3 Capital

Real capital or *economic capital* comprises physical goods that are used in the production of other goods and services. *Financial capital* refers to the funds or money used to purchase real/economic capital (e.g., equipment, for producing goods and services).

In this book, the word *capital* refers to financial capital. The money invested may be referred to as the *asset, capital, principal,* or the *cost basis* of the investment.

Cost of Capital

The *Cost of Capital* (COC) is the *Rate of Return* (ROR) that capital could be expected to earn in an alternative investment of equivalent risk. Therefore, for an investment to be financially palatable, the expected return on capital should be at least the *Cost of Capital*.

The capital structure

A company is typically composed of stakeholders: debt holders (banks, creditors, etc.), equity holders (stockholders). The percentage allocated to each stakeholder class in a company is referred to as the company's *capital structure*. Management must identify the "optimal mix" of financing.

The capital structure of the company is often established so that the *Cost of Capital* is minimized in order that the firm's value is maximized. Generally, when a company invests in an activity or project, the company should expect returns equal to or higher than the company's average *Cost of Capital*.

WACC:

A company's securities typically include both debt and equity, and the cost of debt and equity both factor into the company's *Cost of Capital*. Each stakeholder typically has a different required *Rate of Return*, thus the total *Cost of Capital* for a company is referred to as the *Weighted Average Cost of Capital (WACC)* as defined below:

$$WACC = w_d k_d + w_p k_p + w_c k_c \qquad 1.1$$

Where the following terms are used:

w_d = weight (percentage) of debt,
k_d = rate of return for debt
w_p = weight of preferred stock,
k_p = rate of return for preferred stock
w_c = weight of common stock,
k_c = rate of return for common stock

Example

ABC Corp. is considering investing in an asset costing $10,000 that will be held for one year. ABC's capital structure is made up of 40% debt, 10% preferred stock and 50% common stock. The *Cost of Capital* for debt holders is 7%, for preferred stock is 10% and for common stock is 12%.

Since the capital structure is assumed to be optimal, any new capital raised should be raised in the same proportions as shown in the table.

Source of Funds	Weight	Amount	Rate	Return
Debt	40%	$4,000	7%	$280
Preferred Stock	10%	$1,000	10%	$100
Common Stock	50%	$5,000	12%	$600
				$980

Table 1 WACC example

Thus, the asset must return a minimum of $980 on $10,000 investment or 9.8% return for this to be a viable investment for this particular company.

We can solve for the required *Rate of Return* by using the WACC formula:

$$WACC = (w_p k_p + w_d k_d + w_c k_c)$$
$$= (.40)(.07) + (.10)(.10) + (.50)(.12) = 0.098$$

2 Future and Present Value

2.1 Future Value

The face value of an asset at some point in the future is referred to as its *Future Value (FV)*. The *Future Value* of an asset after one period with *Present Value* PV and *periodic Rate of Return* r is given by

$$FV_1 = PV + PV\,r = PV(1+r) \qquad 2.1$$

The *Future Value* for the kth period is the *Future Value* of the previous period plus the *Rate of Return* for that period given by

$$FV_k = FV_{k-1}(1+r) \qquad 2.2$$

The *Future Value* for the kth period may be expressed in terms of the *Present Value* as

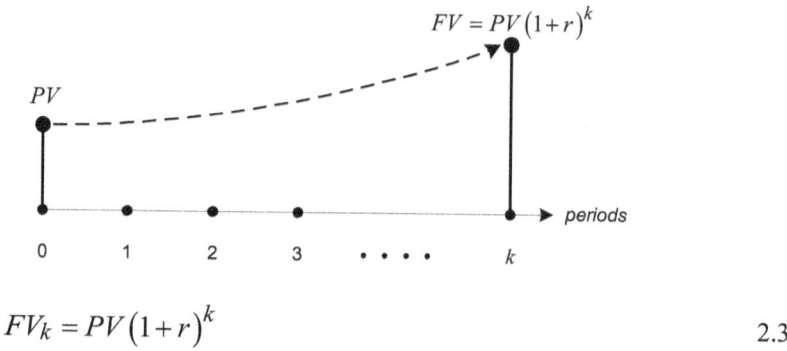

$$FV_k = PV(1+r)^k \qquad 2.3$$

Figure 2-1   Future Value of a sum of money after k years

The following derivation of 2.3 is not a formal proof but it illustrates that the result is true by intuition[1].

The *Future Value* after one year is

$$FV_1 = PV(1+r)$$

The *Future Value* after two years is

$$FV_2 = FV_1(1+r) = PV(1+r)^2$$

The *Future Value* after three years is

$$FV_3 = FV_2(1+r) = PV(1+r)^3$$

Continuing in this fashion we conclude that the *Future Value* after k years is given by

$$FV_k = FV_{k-1}(1+r) = PV(1+r)^k \quad \text{Q.E.D}$$

Example

Consider a one-time investment of $10,000 for a term of 20 years with a nominal interest rate of 10% per year.

$$PV = \$10,000, \quad r = 0.1, \quad n = 20$$

The *Future Value* of the investment after 20 years is

$$FV = PV(1+r)^n = \$10,000(1.1)^{20} = \$67,275$$

---

[1] A formal proof is given in the appendix

2.2 Future Value of a Cash Flow Stream

The *Future Value* of a series of n cash flows with periodic interest r is given by the series.

$$FV = \sum_{i=0}^{k} CF_i (1+r)^{k-i} \qquad \qquad 2.4$$
$$= CF_0(1+r)^k + CF_1(1+r)^{k-1} \ldots CF_n(1+r)^0$$

The *Future Value* of this series of cash flows is illustrated by the following cash flow diagram

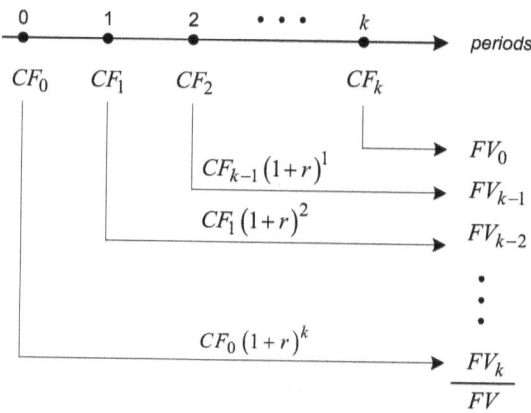

Figure 2-2   Future value of a cash flow stream

Example:

Consider the series of cash flows: 100 in year 0, 200 in year 1 and 50 in year 2 with an annual interest rate of 7%.

$$r = .07, \quad CF_0 = \$100, \quad CF_1 = \$200, \quad CF_2 = \$50$$

The *Future Value* of this cash flow stream after period two is

$$FV = \sum_{i=0}^{2} CF_i(1+r)^{2-i} = \$100(1.07)^2 + \$200(1.07) + \$50 = \$378.48$$

2.3 Present Value

An asset for a payment received in the future can be *discounted* by an appropriate *Discount Rate* (DR or r) to find an equivalent *Present Value* (PV).

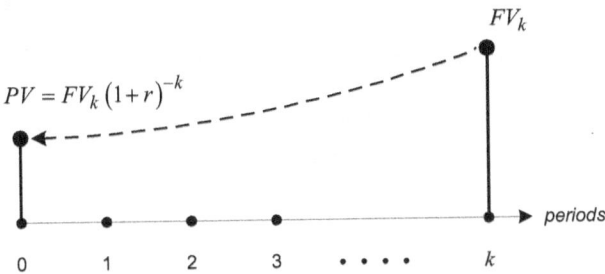

Figure 2-3   Discounting a *Future Value* to *Present Value*

The *Present Value* with *Discount Rate* r can be obtained from a *Future Value* that has accrued over a *term* of k years by

$$PV_k = \frac{FV_k}{(1+r)^k} \qquad 2.5$$

The following example illustrates the fact that discounting a *Future Value* to a *Present Value* is the inverse operation of finding the *Future Value* for a *Present Value*.

Example

Assume a *Present Value* of $10,000 has accumulated after 8 years at an annual interest rate of 7%.

$$PV = 10{,}000, \quad r = .07, \quad n = 8$$

The future value after 8 years is

$$FV = PV(1+r)^k = \$10{,}000(1.07)^8 = \$17{,}181.86$$

Now consider you are presented with an opportunity to receive $17,181.8 eight years from today. What is that investment worth in today's dollars?

$$PV = FV(1+r)^{-k} = \$17{,}181.8(1.07)^{-8} = \$9{,}999.96 \approx \$10{,}000$$

2.4 Present Value of a Cash Flow Stream

The *Present Value* of a stream of cash flows is found by taking the *Present Value* of each element in the series and is given by

$$PV = \sum_{i=0}^{k} \frac{CF_i}{(1+r)^i}$$

$$= CF_0 + \frac{CF_1}{(1+r)} + \frac{CF_2}{(1+r)^2} \ldots + \frac{CF_k}{(1+r)^k}$$

2.6

The *Present Value* of this series of cash flows is illustrated by the following cash flow diagram

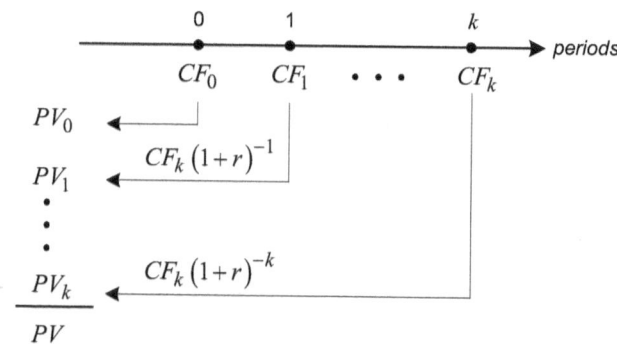

Figure 2-4 *Present Value* of a cash flow stream

Future and Present Value

Example

Given a series of cash flows: 100 in year 0, 200 in year 1, 50 in year 2 with an annual interest rate of 7%:

$$r = .07, \quad CF_0 = \$100, \quad CF_1 = \$200, \quad CF_2 = \$50$$

The *Present Value* of this cash flow stream is

$$\begin{aligned} PV &= \sum_{i=0}^{2} CF_i(1+r)^{-i} \\ &= \$100 + \$200(1.07)^{-1} + \$50(1.07)^{-2} \\ &= \$330.58 \end{aligned}$$

3 Interest

3.1 Simple Interest

When you borrow money, there is normally a fee the lender charges for the use of their money. The fee, referred to as the interest, is expressed as a percentage of the loan per unit time. The original amount loaned is called the *principal*, and the percentage of the principal which must be paid annually as interest is called the *interest rate*.

A *simple interest* is computed only on the original amount borrowed. It is the interest calculated as a simple percentage of the original principal amount. Accumulated interest from future periods is not used in calculations.

The interest on a loan where the principal or *Present Value PV*, interest r percent and k number of periods is given by:

$$Interest = r\,k\,PV \qquad\qquad 3.1$$

The *Future Value* for *simple interest* is

$$FV = PV(1+rk) \qquad\qquad 3.2$$

Example

Assume you invest $1000 today for 5 years at simple interest of $r = 10\%$. You will earn $100 per year in interest. The resulting interest over the five-year term of the loan is

$$FV = \$1,000(1+(0.1)(5)) = \$1,500$$

3.2 Compound Interest

Another method for calculating interest is by compounding the interest. The *compound interest* is calculated each period on the original principal and all interest accumulated during past periods.

Although the interest may be stated as a yearly rate, the *compounding periods* can be yearly, semiannually, quarterly, or continuously. The interest earned in each period is added to the principal of the previous period which then becomes the principal for the next period.

The *Future Value* on a principal (*Present Value*) with compound interest rate of r per period for the kth period is given by

$$FV_k = PV(1+r)^k \qquad 3.3$$

The *Future Value* for interest compounded monthly is

$$FV_k = PV\left(1+\frac{r}{12}\right)^{12k} \qquad 3.4$$

Example

Consider a one-time investment of $10,000 for 20 years with a nominal interest rate of 10%.

$$PV = \$10,000, \quad r = 0.1, \quad n = 20$$

The *FV* after 20 years for *simple* annual interest is

$$FV = PV(1+rn) = \$10,000(1.1)20 = \$30,000$$

The *FV* after 20 years for interest *compounded annually* is

$$FV = PV(1+r)^n = 10,000(1.1)^{20} = 67,275$$

The FV after 20 years for interest *compounded monthly* is

$$FV = PV\left(1+\frac{r}{12}\right)^{n\,12} = \$10000\left(1+\frac{0.1}{12}\right)^{(20)(12)} = \$73,280$$

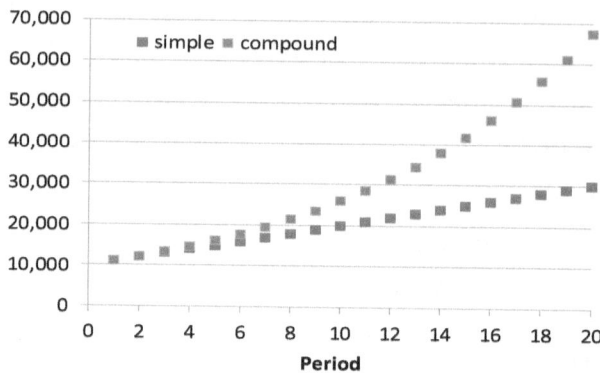

Figure 3-1 Simple vs. compund interest : *rate=10%*, and *i=20* years

3.3 Effective Interest

A *Nominal Annual Interest Rate* is usually the annual interest rate quoted by a lender and is simply the periodic rate multiplied by the number of periods per year.

$$r = im \qquad 3.5$$

Where

  i = periodic interest rate
  m = periods/year

Due to compounding, the actual annual rate is higher than the stated nominal rate. The *Effective Annual Interest Rate* denoted by r_e is the actual interest rate paid in one year divided by the principal for that year, from which

$$r_e = \frac{IntPaid}{PV} = \frac{FV - PV}{PV}$$
$$= \frac{PV\left(1 + \frac{r_n}{m}\right)^m - PV}{PV} = \left(1 + \frac{r_n}{m}\right)^m - 1 \qquad 3.6$$

Where

r_e = effective annual rate
r_n = nominal annual rate
m = periods/year

4 Annuities

4.1 Annuity

An *annuity* is a series of equal cash flows, received by the owner, periodically (evenly) spaced in time. An annuity with a constant payment p starting at year one is illustrated in the following cash flow diagram.

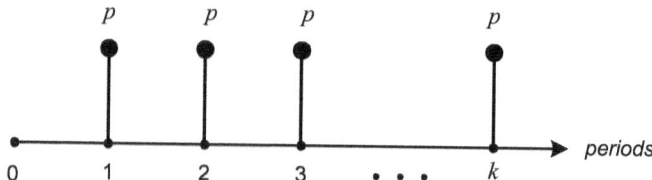

Figure 4-1 Annuity Cashflows

4.2 Present Value of an Annuity

The *Present Value for an annuity* with a constant payment p, nominal rate of r, term of n years and cash flows starting at year (period) one is given by:

$$PV = \sum_{i=1}^{n} \frac{p}{(1+r)^i} = p \frac{1-(1+r)^{-n}}{r} \qquad 4.1$$

Proof:

The *Present Value* for the stream is given by

$$PV = p \sum_{i=1}^{n} \frac{1}{(1+r)^i} = p\left(\alpha^{-1} + \alpha^{-2} \cdots + \alpha^{-n}\right)$$

Where a = 1 + r. Subtracting (a PV) from PV gives

$$PV(\alpha - 1)$$
$$= p\left(\left(\alpha^0 + \alpha^{-1} \cdots + \alpha^{-n+1}\right) - \left(\alpha^{-1} + \alpha^{-2} \cdots + \alpha^{-n+1} + \alpha^{-n}\right)\right)$$
$$= p\left(\alpha^0 - \alpha^{-n}\right) = p\left(1 - \alpha^{-n}\right)$$

Solving for PV and substituting α = 1 + r yields

$$PV = p\frac{1-\alpha^n}{\alpha-1} = p\frac{1-(1+r)^n}{(1+r)-1} = p\frac{1-(1+r)^{-n}}{r} \quad \text{Q.E.D.}$$

Example

Assume we have an investment with an annual (nominal) return of 8% and that we receive $100 per year each year for 5 years as shown in the following cash flow diagram.

$$r = .08, \quad n = 5, \quad p = \$100$$

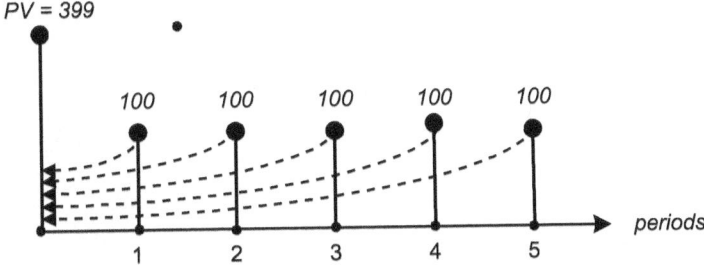

Figure 4-2 Present Value of an Annuity

Solving for the Present Value yields

$$PV = p\frac{1-(1+r)^{-n}}{r} = \$100\frac{1-(1+0.08)^{-5}}{0.08} \approx \$399$$

Therefore, the *Present Value* of this annuity is ≈ $399. This means if we were to deposit $399 dollars into an account that paid 8% annual interest, we could withdraw $100 at the end of each year for the next 5 years and have a balance of $0 at the end of the fifth year.

4.3 Future Value of an Annuity

The *Future Value* for an annuity with a constant payment *p*, nominal rate *r* and cash flows starting at year (period) one is given by

$$FV = \sum_{i=1}^{n} p(1+r)^{n-i} = p\frac{(1+r)^n - 1}{r} \qquad 4.2$$

Proof:

The *Future Value* of the stream is

$$FV = p\sum_{i=1}^{n}(1+r)^{n-i} = p\left(\alpha^{n-1} + \alpha^{n-2} \cdots + \alpha + 1\right)$$

Where α = 1 + *r*. Multiplying the series *FV* by α, yields

$$\alpha FV = p\left(\alpha^n + \cdots + \alpha^2 + \alpha\right)$$

Subtracting *FV* from α *FV* gives

$$FV(\alpha - 1) = p\left(\left(\alpha^n + \cdots + \alpha^2 + \alpha\right) - \left(\alpha^{n-1} + \alpha^{n-2} \cdots + \alpha + 1\right)\right)$$
$$= p\left(\alpha^n - 1\right)$$

Solving for *FV* and substituting α = 1 + *r* gives

$$FV = p\frac{\alpha^n - 1}{\alpha - 1} = p\frac{(1+r)^n - 1}{(1+r) - 1} = p\frac{(1+r)^n - 1}{r} \qquad \text{Q.E.D}$$

Example

Assume you deposit $100 each year into an IRA which earns 8% interest for 10 years. Find the *Future Value* of the account at the end of year 10.

$$r = .08, \quad n = 10, \quad p = 100$$

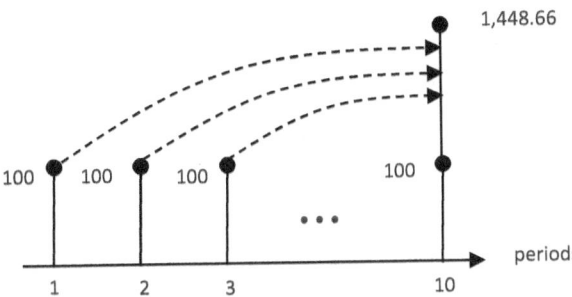

Figure 4-3

Solving for the *Future Value* yields

$$FV = \frac{p((1+r)^n - 1)}{r} = \frac{\$100((1+.08)^{10} - 1)}{.08} = \$1,448.66$$

Example

For the annuity in the previous example solve for the *Present Value* from either the *Future Value* or from the cash flow stream.

The *Present Value* obtained from the *Future Value* using eq 2.5 is

$$PV = \frac{FV}{(1+r)^n} = \frac{\$1,448.66}{(1+.08)^{10}} \approx \$671 \tag{2.5}$$

The *Present Value* obtained by equation 4.1 from the individual cash flows is

$$PV = \frac{p\left(1-(1+r)^{-n}\right)}{r} = \frac{\$100\left(1-(1+.08)^{-10}\right)}{.08} \approx \$671 \qquad (4.1)$$

Both methods lead to the same value of ≈ $671. Thus, if we were to invest $671 at a rate of 8% for 10 years, we should be left with ≈ $1,448 at the end of the year 10.

$$FV = PV(1+r)^n = \$671(1+.08)^{10} \approx \$1,448$$

4.4 Payment and Term of an Annuity

If we are given the rate, term and either *Present Value* or *Future Value* of an annuity, we can solve for the required payment.

The annuity payment *p* as a function of *PV* is

$$p = rPV\frac{(1+r)^n}{(1+r)^n - 1} \qquad (4.3)$$

The annuity payment *p* as a function of *FV* is

$$p = rFV\frac{1}{(1+r)^n - 1} \qquad (4.4)$$

Proof:

The proof of (4.3) *p* as a function of *PV* is given here. The proof of (4.3)(4.4) for *p* as a function of *FV* is similar.

Given equation 4.1

$$PV = p\frac{1-(1+r)^{-n}}{r} \qquad (4.1)$$

Annuities

Solving for p gives

$$p = rPV \frac{1}{\left(1-(1+r)^{-n}\right)(1+r)^n} \frac{(1+r)^n}{(1+r)^n} = rPV \frac{(1+r)^n}{(1+r)^n - (1+r)^{-n+n}}$$

$$= rPV \frac{(1+r)^n}{(1+r)^n - (1+r)^0} = rPV \frac{(1+r)^n}{(1+r)^n - 1} \quad \text{Q.E.D.}$$

If we are given the rate, payment and either *Present Value* or *Future Value* of an annuity, we can solve for the required term.

The annuity term *n* as a function of *PV* is

$$n = -\frac{Log\left(1 - PV\frac{r}{p}\right)}{Log(1+r)} \quad (4.5)$$

The annuity term *n* as a function of *FV* is

$$n = \frac{Log\left(1 + FV\frac{r}{p}\right)}{Log(1+r)} \quad (4.6)$$

Proof:

The proof of equation (4.5) for *n* as a function of *PV* is given here. The proof of equation (4.6) for *n* as a function of *FV* is similar.

Given equation 4.1

$$PV = p \frac{\left(1-(1+r)^{-n}\right)}{r} \quad (4.1)$$

Multiply both sides by r/p, next subtract 1 from each side and then multiply both sides by -1 which yields

$$1 - \frac{r}{p}PV = (1+r)^{-n}$$

Take the Log of both sides

$$Log\left(1 - \frac{r}{p}PV\right) = -n Log(1+r)$$

Solving for n gives

$$n = -\frac{Log\left(1 - \frac{r}{p}PV\right)}{Log(1+r)} \quad \text{Q.E.D.}$$

Example

Assume an annuity with n = 5, r = 4% and *Future Value* of $10,000. What is the annual payment?

Solution:

The payment is

$$p = FV \frac{r}{(1+r)^n - 1} = \frac{\$10,000(.04)}{(1+.04)^5 - 1} \approx \$1,846$$

Example

Assume you can afford to pay $1,846 per year. You want to accumulate a *Future Value* of $10,000. How many years will it take?

Solution:

$$n = \frac{Log\left(1 + FV\frac{r}{p}\right)}{Log(1+r)} = \frac{Log\left(1 + \$10,000 \frac{.04}{\$1,846}\right)}{Log(1+.04)} = 5$$

It will take 5 years to accumulate $10,000, as confirmed in the previous example.

5 Mortgages

5.1 Mortgages

A *mortgage* represents a loan or lien on an asset such as a property or house that has to be paid over a specified period of time. The monthly payment to the loan's interest and principal is called an *amortization schedule*. With most loans you pay off the interest on the loan before you pay off the principal. The payment amount is calculated so as to pay off the entire loan in a specified number of payments referred to as the *term of the loan*.

A typical loan operates as follows:

(1) You borrow the initial amount, principal (Present Value) denoted P_0 with a term of n and periodic rate of r.

(2) At the end of each payment period, you pay the periodic payment amount denoted by p.

(3) The periodic payment is applied first to interest owed on the remaining balance.

(4) The remaining part of the payment is applied to reduce the principal. The outstanding principal after the kth payment is denoted by P_k

5.2 Remaining Principal

The remaining principal at the end of the kth year is given by

$$P_k = P_0(1+r)^k - p\frac{(1+r)^k - 1}{r} \qquad 5.1$$

Where:

P_k = principal owed at the end of the kth year
P_0 = initial pricipal
r = periodic interest rate
p = periodic payment

Proof:

At the end of the kth period (prior to payment) the outstanding debt increases by the interest on the previous principal P_{k-1}. Thus, the principal at the end of the kth period after the payment is made is

$$P_k = \alpha P_{k-1} - p$$

Where $\alpha = 1+r$. Substituting $\alpha P_{k-2} - p$ for P_{k-1} yields

$$P_k = \alpha^2 P_{k-2} - \alpha p - p$$

Substituting $\alpha P_{k-3} - p$ for P_{k-2} yields

$$P_k = \alpha^3 P_{k-3} - \alpha^2 p - p$$

Continuing in this manner we eventually reach the end of the recursion

$$P_k = \alpha^k P_0 - p\left(1 + \alpha + \alpha^2 \cdots + \alpha^{k-1}\right)$$

Now the series $s = 1 + \alpha + \alpha^2 \cdots + \alpha^{(k-1)}$ can be expressed in closed form as

$$s = \sum_{i=0}^{k-1} \alpha^i = \frac{1 - \alpha^{(k-1)+1}}{1-\alpha} = \frac{\alpha^k - 1}{\alpha - 1}$$

Substituting the closed form expression for the series P_k gives

$$P_k = \alpha^k P_0 - p \frac{\alpha^k - 1}{\alpha - 1}$$

Substituting $\alpha = 1 + r$ and $P_0 = PV$ gives the principal owed for the kth period.

$$P_k = (1+r)^k PV - p \frac{(1+r)^k - 1}{r} \quad \text{Q.E.D}$$

5.3 Loan, Payments and Periods

Given a mortgage with a term of n periods and interest rate of r, we can solve for the principal or number of periods or loan amount by setting $P_k = 0$ and solving for the variable of interest.

$$PV = \frac{p\left(1 - (1+r)^{-k}\right)}{r} \qquad 5.2$$

$$p = PV \frac{r(1+r)^k}{-1 + (1+r)^k} \qquad 5.3$$

$$k = -\frac{\mathrm{Log}\left(1 - PV \frac{r}{p}\right)}{\mathrm{Log}(1+r)} \qquad 5.4$$

Example

Given a loan with the following parameters:

PV	=	$150,000	principle
R	=	.07	annual rate
m	=	12	periods per year
$r = R/m$	=	.0058	periodic rate
n	=	15	years
$k = mn$	=	180	periods

The *monthly payments* are:

$$p = PV \frac{r(1+r)^k}{-1+(1+r)^k} = \$150{,}000 \frac{.0058(1+.0058)^{180}}{-1+(1+.0058)^{180}} = \$1{,}348.24$$

The *principal* after the 15th year (180 periods), P_{180} should be zero

$$P_n = PV(1+r)^k - \frac{p\left((1+r)^k - 1\right)}{r}$$

$$= \$150{,}000(1+.0058)^{180} - \frac{\$1{,}348.24\left((1+.0058)^{180} - 1\right)}{.0058} = 0$$

The *payment to interest* in the kth period denoted ip_k is equal to the outstanding principal at the $(k-1)^{th}$ period, times the periodic interest rate r.

$$ip_k = r\, P_{k-1} = -\left((1+r)^{k-1} pv - p \frac{(1+r)^{k-1} - 1}{r}\right) r \qquad 5.5$$

The *payment to principal* in the kth period denoted as pp_k is equal the payment minus the interest paid at the kth period

$$pp_k = p - ip_k \qquad 5.6$$

Example

Given a loan with the following parameters, determine the required loan amount.

p	=	$1,348	payment
R	=	.07	annual rate
m	=	12	periods per year
$r = R/m$	=	.0058	periodic rate
n	=	15	years
$k = mn$	=	180	periods

Solution:

$$PV = \frac{p(1+r)^{-k}\left((1+r)^k - 1\right)}{r}$$

$$= \frac{\$1{,}348(1+.0058)^{-180}\left((1+.0058)^{180} - 1\right)}{.0058}$$

$$= \$150{,}347$$

Example

Given a loan with the following parameters, determine the required term

p	=	$1,348	payment
R	=	.07	annual rate
m	=	12	periods per year
$r = R/m$	=	.0058	periodic rate
PV	=	$150,000	loan

Mortgages

Solution:

The number of periods required to pay off the loan is

$$k = -\frac{Log\left(1-\frac{rPV}{P}\right)}{Log(1+r)} = -\frac{Log\left(1-\frac{(.0058)(150,000)}{1,348}\right)}{Log(1+0.0058)} = 180 \text{ periods}$$

The number of years required to pay off the loan is

$$n = \frac{k}{m} = \frac{180}{12} = 15 \text{ years}$$

Example

Given a loan in the previous section with the following parameters, determine the amount paid to interest and principal at period 15

PV	=	$150,000	principle
R	=	.07	annual rate
m	=	12	periods per year
r = R/m	=	.0058	periodic rate
n	=	15	years
k = mn	=	180	periods

Solution:

The payment to interest for the kth period is

$$ip_k = r P_{k-1} = -\left((1+r)^{k-1} pv - p\frac{(1+r)^{k-1}-1}{r}\right) r$$

From which for the 15th period is

$$ip_{15} = -.0058\left(\$150,000(1+.0058)^{14} - \$1,348\frac{(1+.0058)^{14}-1}{.0058}\right)$$

$$= \$1,064$$

The payment to principal for the 15th period is

$$pp_{15} = p - ip_{15} = \$1,348.24 - \$1,064 = \$284.63$$

Example

Given a loan in with the following parameters we generate an amortization table showing the progression of principal and payment to interest and principal over the course of the loan.

PV	=	$\$10,000$	principle
m	=	1	periods per year
$r = R$	=	.07	periodic = annual rate
$n = k$	=	10	years = periods

Solution:

The monthly payments are

$$p = PV \frac{r(1+r)^k}{-1+(1+r)^k} = \$10,000 \frac{.07(1+.07)^{10}}{-1+(1+.07)^{10}} = \$1,423.78$$

The amortization table for this example is shown below

Year	Principal	Payments	Pay2Int	Pay2Prin
1	9276	1423.78	649.32	774.455
2	8501	1423.78	595.07	828.705
3	7673	1423.78	537.11	886.665
4	6786	1423.78	475.02	948.755
5	5837	1423.78	408.59	1015.19
6	4822	1423.78	337.54	1086.24
7	3736	1423.78	261.52	1162.26
8	2574	1423.78	180.18	1243.6
9	1330	1423.78	93.1	1330.68
10	0	1423.78	0	1423.78

Table 2   Amortization Table

6 NPV, IRR and MIRR

6.1 Net Present Value (NPV)

The *Net Present Value (NPV)* is used in *capital budgeting* to analyze the profitability of an investment or project. The *initial outlay* or *initial offering* (*IO*) represents the initial net cost of an investment and the *NPV* of an investment represents the excess value (above the initial outlay). So, the *NPV* may be expressed as

$$NPV = PV - IO = Value - Cost \qquad 6.1$$

The initial investment (*IO*) is sometimes designated as cash flow zero or CF_0. The NPV of the investment is equal to the Present Value of future cash flows minus the initial offering (IO).

$$NPV = \sum_{i=0}^{n} \frac{CF_i}{(1+r)^i} \quad \text{where} \quad CF_0 = -IO \qquad 6.2$$

The following figure illustrates the concept of NPV. The initial offering is negative (cash out) and the PV of future cash flows are positive (cash in).

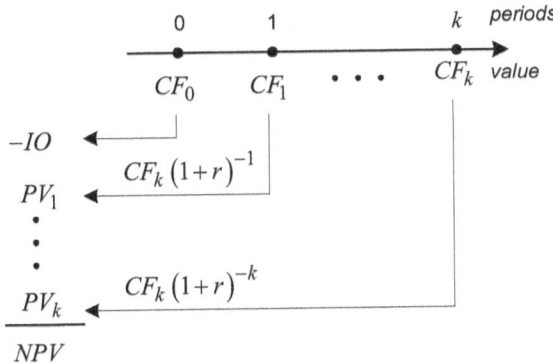

Figure 6-1   NPV of a series of cash flows

A positive NPV represents a net gain in wealth while a negative NPV represents a loss in wealth. For two mutually exclusive investments choose the one with a higher positive NPV.

Example

The IO of an investment is 100. The Cost of Capital (COC) or Discount Rate (DR) is 10%. The investment generates cash flows of 10, 60 and 80 dollars in years 1, 2 and 3 respectively as depicted in the following figure.

$$r = 0.1, \quad IO = \$100, \quad CF_1 = \$10, \quad CF_2 = \$60, \quad CF_3 = \$80$$

The NPV is for this investment is

$$NPV = \sum_{i=1}^{3} CF_i (1+r)^{-i} - IO$$
$$= \$10(1.1)^{-1} + \$60(1.1)^{-2} + \$80(1.1)^{-3} - \$100$$
$$= 9.09 + 49.59 + 60.11 - 100 = \$18.79$$

The cash flows are

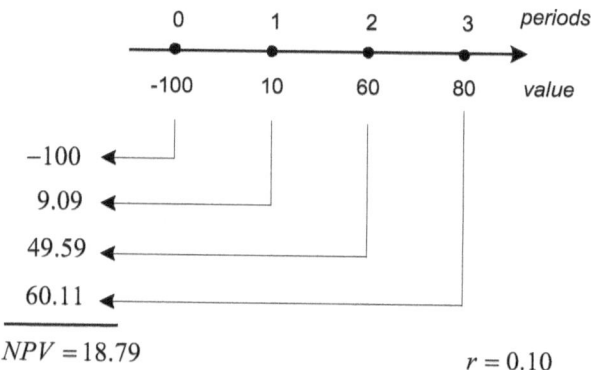

Figure 6-2

6.2 Internal Rate of Return (*IRR*)

The Internal Rate of Return (IRR) provides a measure of the average annual Rate of Return for an investment. The IRR is defined as the Discount Rate which makes the Present Value of cash flows zero.

$$NPV(IRR) = 0 \qquad 6.3$$

In other words, the IRR is the Discount Rate *r* that equates Present Value of cash flows with initial outlay.

$$PV(IRR) = IO \qquad 6.4$$

The IRR suffers from several problems that can lead to sub-optimal decisions.

(1) Implicit in the calculations of the IRR is the assumption that cash flows are reinvested at the IRR rate. In many cases with investments involving a very high or low IRR may be unrealistic and can lead to incorrect results (see reinvestment rate assumption in the following section)

(2) To solve for the IRR, one must determine the discount rate that makes the net present value zero. However, this requires knowing the IRR itself — the very quantity being sought. For this reason, the IRR cannot usually be solved algebraically and must instead be found iteratively by starting with an initial guess and refining it numerically. In some cases, multiple IRR solutions may exist for the same set of cash flows.

(3) The NPV always leads to an economically correct decision when choosing between investments while the *IRR* may not.

The *IRR* must be solved numerically. One suitable technique is the Newton-method. Given a function of a real variable f(x), the Newton-Raphson method iteratively finds the ith root z_i such that $f(z_i) = 0$.

Given $z_i(k)$ is the estimate of the ith root at the kth iteration. The Newton-Raphson method provides an improved estimate for the $k+1$ iteration z_{k+1}.

The new estimate is based on the following recursion

$$x_{k+1} = x_k - \frac{f(x_k)}{f'(x_k)} \quad\quad 6.5$$

Where

$$f(x_k) = f(x = x_k),$$
$$f'(x_k) = \frac{d}{dx} f(x = x_k)$$

Example

Find the IRR for the following cash flows

$$CF_0 = -\$30, \quad CF_1 = \$20, \quad CF_2 = \$30, \quad CF_3 = \$10$$

Solution:

The NPV(r) and NPV'(r) are given by:

$$NPV(r) = -\$30 + \frac{\$20}{(1+r)} + \frac{\$30}{(1+r)^2} + \frac{\$10}{(1+r)^3}$$

$$NPV'(r) = -\frac{\$20}{(1+r)^2} - \frac{\$60}{(1+r)^3} - \frac{\$30}{(1+r)^4}$$

For an initial guess, try $r = 0.2$. The first iteration is shown below.

$$r_1 = .2 - \frac{-\$30 + \frac{\$20}{(1+.2)} + \frac{\$30}{(1+.2)^2} + \frac{\$10}{(1+.2)^3}}{-\frac{\$20}{(1+.2)^2} - \frac{\$60}{(1+.2)^3} - \frac{\$30}{(1+.2)^4}} = 0.41064 \quad\quad 6.6$$

NPV, IRR and MIRR

Now using r_1 as a new guess, the second iteration is

$$r_2 = .41064 - \frac{-\$30 + \dfrac{\$20}{(1+.41064)} + \dfrac{\$30}{(1+.41064)^2} + \dfrac{\$10}{(1+.41064)^3}}{-\dfrac{\$20}{(1+.41064)^2} - \dfrac{\$60}{(1+.41064)^3} - \dfrac{\$30}{(1+.41064)^4}}$$

$$= 0.482856$$

Continuing in like fashion the next 3 iterations indicates that the process has converged

$$r_3 = 0.488726,\ r_4 = 0.48876,\ r_5 = 0.48876$$

From which

$$IRR = 48.876\%$$

Example

Find the IRR for the following cash flows

$$CF_0 = -\$50,\quad CF_1 = \$20,\quad CF_2 = \$30,\quad CF_3 = \$10$$

Solution:

The $NPV(r)$ and $NPV(r)'$ are given below:

$$NPV(r) = -\$50 + \frac{\$20}{(1+r)} + \frac{\$30}{(1+r)^2} + \frac{\$10}{(1+r)^3}$$

$$NPV'(r) = -\frac{\$20}{(1+r)^2} - \frac{\$60}{(1+r)^3} - \frac{\$30}{(1+r)^4}$$

For an initial guess try $r = 0.05$. The first three iterations are shown below and have converged.

$$r_1 = 0.105948,\ r_2 = 0.105997,\ r_3 = 0.105997$$

From which

$$IRR = 10.59\%$$

6.3 Modified Internal Rate of Return (MIRR)

In order to avoid potential errors using the *IRR*, investor can instead use a *Modified Internal Rate of Return (MIRR)*. Calculating the Present Value of a future cash flow assumes that the cash flows are reinvested at a discount rate *r* typically the companies *Cost of Capital (COC)*.

This is a subtle fact and has escaped many even financial professionals. This subtlety is the key in understanding the difference between the *Internal Rate of Return (IRR)* and *Modified Internal Rate of Return (MIRR)*.

To see that the reinvestment assumption is true consider the following simple example. We have a single cash flow at year *k* denoted as CF_k. We begin by calculating the *PV* of this cash flow directly, denoted by PV_A

$$PV_A = \frac{CF_k}{(1+r)^k} \qquad 6.7$$

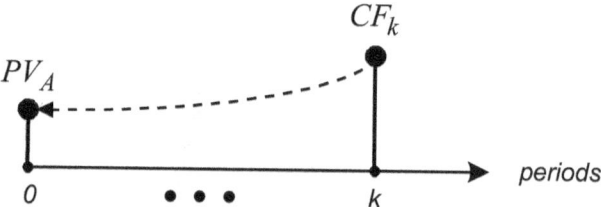

Figure 6-3

Now instead of discounting CF_k back to *PV* directly, let's first project this cash flow out to its Future Value for year *n* assuming periodic interest *r*

$$FV_n = CF_k(1+r)^{n-k} \qquad 6.8$$

We can discount the *Future Value* back to *Present Value* which we denote PV_B. The process of projecting out to *FV* and then discounting to *PV* is shown in the following figure.

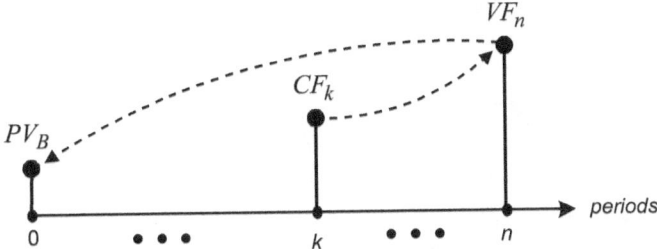

Figure 6-4

The value of PV_B is given by

$$PV_B = \frac{FV_n}{(1+r)^n} = \frac{CF_1(1+r)^{n-k}}{(1+r)^n} = \frac{CF_k}{(1+r)^k} = PV_A \quad \text{Q.E.D} \qquad 6.9$$

Since $PV_A = PV_B$, it shows that calculating the *Present Value* of a cash flow at year k is equivalent to projecting the *Future Value* of the cash flow to year n and reinvesting each year at a rate r. The following section describes the implications of this result.

Consider a company with a *Cost of Capital* (*WACC*) of 8% that is evaluating a potential project. Assume that the *IRR* for the project is determined to be 35%.

Implicit in the *IRR* is the assumption (eq 6.9) that any money from this project is reinvested at a rate of 35% instead of the *Cost of Capital* of 8%. Thus, the *IRR* would lead to an *artificially high* expectations for the return.

To avoid problems with the *IRR* we can use a *Modified Internal Rate of Return* (*MIRR*). The *MIRR* is the *Discount Rate* which makes the *Present Value* of future cash flows zero.

The cash flow diagram for calculating the *Modified Internal Rate of Return* (*MIRR*) is shown below.

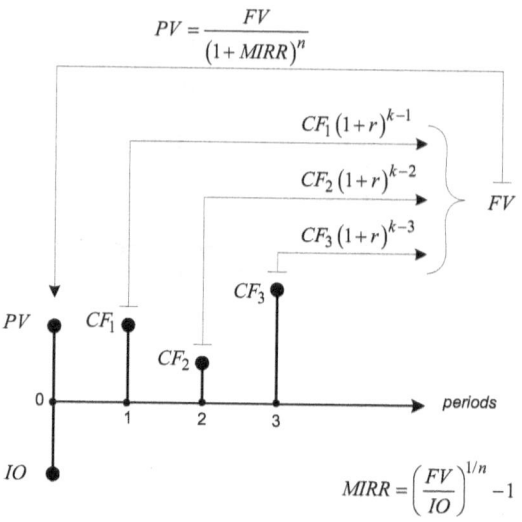

Figure 6-5   Modified Internal Rate of Return (MIRR)

Unlike the *IRR* the *MIRR* allows you to *specify the reinvestment rate* of future cash flows over the holding period. Since the *MIRR* allows you to specify the reinvestment rate at the firm's *Cost of Capital* *(COC)*, it more accurately reflects the profitability of a project.

Thus, the *MIRR* always agrees with the *NPV* in terms of choosing between investments, while the *IRR* may or may not agree with the *NPV*.

The *MIRR* is given by

$$MIRR = \left(\frac{FV}{IO}\right)^{1/n} - 1 \qquad 6.10$$

NPV, IRR and MIRR

Proof:

Let r be the reinvestment rate. The *Future Value* of the cash flow stream is found by assuming the reinvestment rate r is equal to the *Cost of Capital*, that is $r = WACC$

$$FV = \sum_{i=1}^{n} CF_i (1+r)^{n-i}$$

The *Present Value* of the *Future Value* is discounted using the *MIRR*

$$PV = \frac{FV}{(1+MIRR)^n}$$

Setting $PV = IO$ and solving for *MIRR* gives

$$MIRR = \left(\frac{FV}{IO}\right)^{1/n} - 1 \quad Q.E.D.$$

Example

ABC Corp. has a *Cost of Capital (COC)* of 10%. It is considering the purchase of an investment for $30. The cash flow in year 1 is $20, year 2 is $30 and year 3 is $10.

$$r = 0.1, \quad \$IO = 30, \quad CF_1 = \$20, \quad CF_2 = \$30, \quad CF_3 = \$10$$

The *Future Value* of the cash flows is

$$FV = \sum_{i=1}^{3} CF_i(1+r)^{3-i} = \$20(1.1)^2 + \$30(1.1)^1 + \$10 = \$67.2$$

The *MIRR* is 30.8%

$$MIRR = \left(\frac{FV}{IO}\right)^{1/3} - 1 = \left(\frac{\$67.2}{\$30}\right)^{1/3} - 1 = 0.3084$$

The PV of the cash flows is

$$PV = \frac{FV}{(1+MIRR)^3} = \frac{\$67.2}{(1+.3083)^3} = \$30$$

Thus, the PV is equal to the initial outlay (IO), so the NPV is zero as expected.

$$NPV = PV - IO = \$30 - \$30 = 0$$

However, the *IRR* for the same scenario is found to be 49% compared with an *MIRR* of 31%. The *IRR* is higher than the *MIRR* by 18% (an error of 63%), because the *IRR* implicitly assumes the cash flows will be reinvested at a return of 49% instead of the true *Cost of Capital (COC)* of 10%, thereby giving an overly optimistic estimate of the investments return.

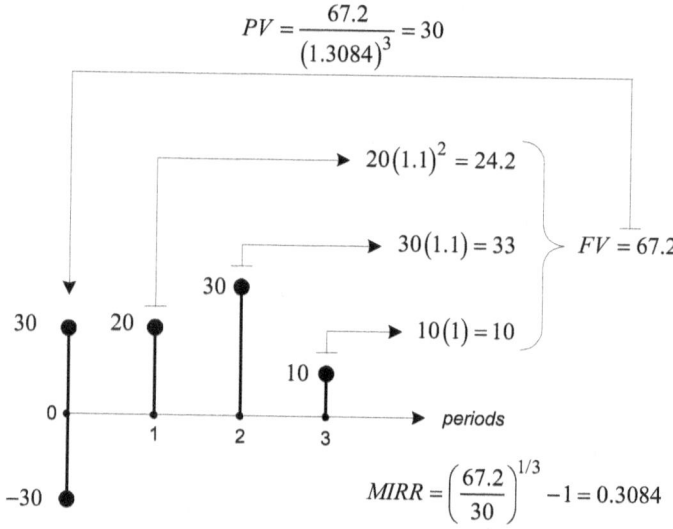

Figure 6-6   MIRR

7 Discounting

7.1 Discount Rate

A *Discount Rate (DR)* is a rate used of return used to convert anticipated future payments or receipts into Present Value (PV) (i.e., the value today, or as of a specified valuation date). Economically, the discount rate represents the required rate of return or the market yield for investments of comparable risk, reflecting the opportunity cost of capital

We may discount a stream of future cash flows to present value using equation 2.6 by substituting by substituting the Discount Rate (DR) for the interest rate r. Future cash flows may occur at different times and may be either positive (cash inflow) or negative (cash outflow).

$$PV = \sum_{i=1}^{k} \frac{CF_i}{(1+DR)^i} \qquad 2.6$$

Example

Assume we are valuing a bond for which a risk rating has been estimated with the following assumptions:

(1) The bond has a face value of $1,000.
(2) It pays 8% interest on its face value.
(3) The bond pays interest once a year, at the end of the year.
(4) The bond matures exactly three years from the valuation date.
(5) As of the valuation date, the yield for bonds of equal risk is 10%.

The *Present Value* of the bond is

$$PV = \frac{\$80}{(1+0.1)^1} + \frac{\$80}{(1+0.1)^2} + \frac{\$80}{(1+0.1)^3} + \frac{\$1000}{(1+0.1)^3} = \$950.263.$$

Note that the bond's coupon rate is 8% while the market yield for bonds of comparable risk is 10%. Because the bond pays a lower interest rate than the market currently requires, investors will only purchase it at a price below its face value.

Accordingly, the bond trades at approximately $950.26, which is less than its $1,000 face value. The bond therefore trades at a discount.

If you purchase the bond for $950.26, the total return you earn will be 10%, which is exactly the market yield required for that level of risk. Although the bond pays only 8% interest on its face value, the investor also earns a capital gain because the bond will be repaid at $1,000 at maturity. The combination of the coupon payments and this capital gain produces the 10% yield.

General Bond Pricing Rule

A bond's price depends on the relationship between its coupon rate and the market yield required for bonds of similar risk.

- If the coupon rate is less than the market yield, the bond sells at a discount (price below face value).
- If the coupon rate equals the market yield, the bond sells at par (price equal to face value).
- If the coupon rate is greater than the market yield, the bond sells at a premium (price above face value).

In this example, the coupon rate is 8% while the market yield is 10%, so the bond sells at a discount below its $1,000 face value, at approximately $950.26.

7.2 Capitalization and Constant Growth

Consider an asset with returns that grow at a constant rate in perpetuity from the period immediately preceding the valuation date as illustrated in the following cash flow diagram

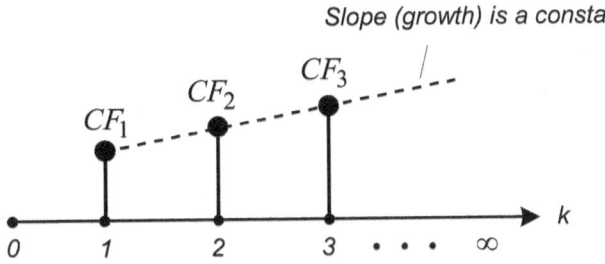

Figure 7-1 Constant Growth

The *growth rate (GR)* of an investment represents the percentage increase of the investment. A *constant growth rate* model, sometimes referred to as *Gordon's Growth Model*, assumes the growth rate from period to period is a constant. When the growth rate (GR) is less than the *Discount Rate (DR)* we may express the *Present Value* in closed-form as

$$PV = CF_0 \frac{(1+GR)}{DR-GR} \qquad \text{(constant growth)} \qquad 7.1$$

Where $GR < DR$ and $GR = $ constant growth

Proof

The *Present Value* of an asset with constant growth rate (GR) and Discount Rate (DR) is given by

$$PV = \frac{CF_1}{(1+DR)} + \frac{CF_2}{(1+DR)^2} + \cdots + \frac{CF_\infty}{(1+DR)^\infty}$$

$$= \frac{CF_0(1+GR)}{(1+DR)} + \frac{CF_0(1+GR)^2}{(1+DR)^2} + \cdots + \frac{CF_0(1+GR)^\infty}{(1+DR)^\infty}$$

CF_0 is the cash flow at the end of the most recent period prior to the valuation date

Substituting $\alpha = (1+GR) / (1+DR)$ gives

$$PV = CF_0\left(\alpha + \alpha^2 + \alpha^3 \cdots + \alpha^\infty\right) = CF_0 \frac{\alpha}{1-\alpha} \qquad 7.2$$

Where we have used the identity:

$$\sum_{i=1}^{\infty} \alpha^i = \frac{\alpha}{1-\alpha} \quad \text{for } |a| < 1$$

Upon substituting $\alpha = (1+GR)/(1+DR)$ in equation 7.2 yields

$$PV = CF_0 \frac{\frac{(1+GR)}{(1+DR)}}{1 - \frac{(1+GR)}{(1+DR)}} = CF_0 \frac{(1+GR)}{(1+DR)-(1+GR)}$$

$$= CF_0 \frac{1+GR}{DR-GR} \qquad \text{Q.E.D}$$

The denominator of the Present Value formula (DR-GR) for constant growth can be represented by a single constant referred to as the *Capitalization Rate (CR)*.

Valuing an investment using a capitalization rate is known as *capitalization*. Also noting that $CF_1 = CF_0 (1+GR)$, the Present Value formula for constant growth may also be given by

$$PV = \frac{CF_1}{CR} \qquad \text{(capitalization)} \qquad 7.3$$

Where CR = DR - GR, CF1 = CF0 (1 + GR) and GR < DR. For constant growth, the equivalence of discounting and capitalization is demonstrated in the following example.

Example

Assume a cash flow in period 1 of $100, growing in perpetuity at 3%. The Cost of Capital (Discount Rate) is 13%. The capitalization rate of 10% is obtained by subtracting the growth rate (GR) from the Discount Rate (DR).

$$DR = 0.13, \ GR = 0.03, \ CF_1 = \$100, \ CR = (DR - GR) = .10$$

Capitalizing the first period cash flow of $100 gives a PV of

$$PV = \frac{CF_1}{CR} = \frac{\$100}{0.1} = \$1,000$$

Now let's check to see if the same result holds for discounting. The following summation is calculated for 80 terms giving a value of $999.9.

$$PV = \sum_{i=1}^{80} CF_1 \frac{(1+GR)^{i-1}}{(1+DR)^i} \approx \$1,000$$

The more terms we include in the summation the closer the Present Value will get to $1,000

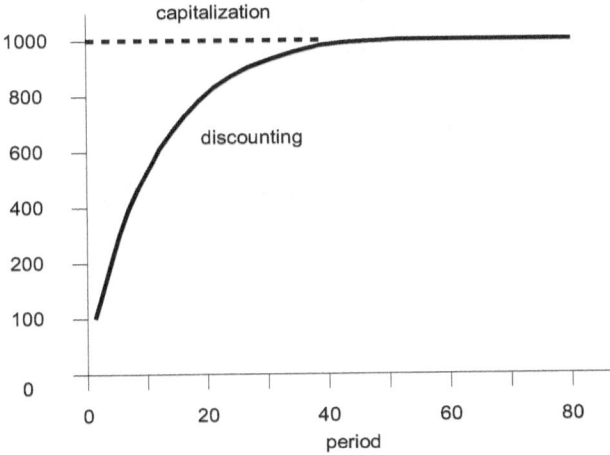

Figure 7-2   Convergence of discounting

7.3 Two Stage Growth Model

The following example illustrates a particularly common type of investment scenario. Assume you are to purchase a business. This business may have a good estimate for near term growth, say 1 to 5 years based on historical trends, new products launches, etc. However, it is unlikely that specific growth far into the future can be predicted with certainty.

Although they may not be able to specify the exact growth rates they are often able to estimate an expected long-term growth rate based on average historical growth, market trends etc. Typically, long-term growth should be based on a *conservative* estimate.

In order to deal with this type of problem we can apply a discrete discounting model to the near-term forecast and apply a capitalization model for the long-term forecast. This model is referred to as a *two-stage growth model* and is illustrated in the following diagram.

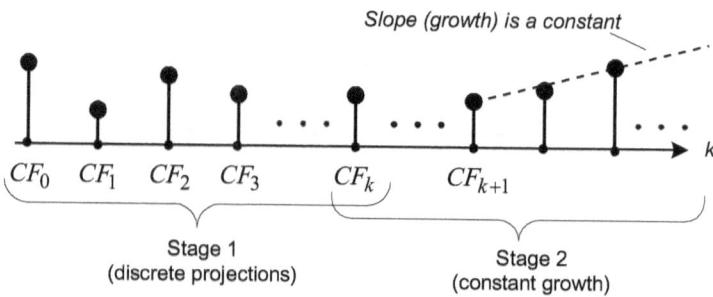

Figure 7-3   Two-stage growth model

Discounting

Stage-1 is the *holding period* or *discrete projection period* representing the period with individual projections for each year from 1 to k.

Stage-2 represents the remaining years characterized by a constant growth rate in perpetuity.

In stage-1 each period's discrete cash flow is discounted to a *Present Value*. The *capitalized value* of the projected cash flows following the end of the discrete projection period is also discounted back to a *Present Value*.

The sum of the *Present Values* for stages-1 and stage-2 is the total *Present Value*. The capitalized value of the projected cash flows following the discrete projection period is called the *terminal value* or *residual value*.

Note that stage-1 and stage-2 overlap by one period. "*The assumption made is that the kth period cash flow CF_k is received at the end of the kth period, that is, the investment could be sold at the end of the kth period.*

The end of the kth period is also the beginning of the $k+1^{th}$ period, so they must be discounted for the same number of periods" [Pratt, 1970].

The *Present Value* for a two-stage model is given by the following.

$$PV = \underbrace{\frac{CF_1}{(1+DR)^1} \cdots + \frac{CF_n}{(1+DR)^n}}_{\text{stage 1}} + \underbrace{\frac{\frac{CF_n(1+GR)}{(DR-GR)}}{(1+DR)^n}}_{\text{stage 2}} \qquad 7.4$$

Example

Consider an investment with the following parameters:

(1) Expected net cash flows for years 1, 2, and 3 are $100, $120, and $140, respectively.

(2) Beyond year 3, cash flow is expected to grow fairly evenly at a rate of about 5% in perpetuity.

(3) The Cost of Capital is estimated to be 12%.

Given

$$CF_1 = \$100, \quad CF_2 = \$120, \quad CF_3 = \$140, \quad DR = 0.12, \quad GR = 0.05$$

The terminal value is

$$TV_3 = CF_3 \frac{(1+GR)}{(DR-GR)} = 140 \frac{(1.05)}{(0.12-0.05)} = \$2,100$$

The Present Value of the investment is

$$PV = \frac{100}{(1.12)^1} + \frac{120}{(1.12)^2} + \frac{140}{(1.12)^3} + \frac{\$2,100}{(1.12)^3} \approx \$1,779$$

Thus, the estimated value is $1,779. This is the price a willing buyer would expect to pay for this investment.

8 Appendix (optional)

This appendix presents an optional proof of equation 2.3. The result itself is standard in finance texts, where the future value formula is typically introduced directly without proof. However, many readers—particularly those with backgrounds in engineering, mathematics, or the sciences—may appreciate seeing how the formula follows from a simple mathematical argument.

The proof uses mathematical induction, a standard technique from number theory and abstract algebra. While this level of rigor is not necessary for understanding the financial concepts discussed in this document, it illustrates the mathematical structure underlying compound growth.

Readers interested primarily in the practical application of the formulas may safely skip this section.

Axiom of Induction:

Let each $n \in \mathbb{N} = \{1, 2, \ldots\}$ where $\mathbb{N}$ is the set of natural numbers be associated with a statement $P(n)$ which is either true or false. Then $P(n)$ is true $\forall n \in \mathbb{N}$ if the following conditions (1) and (2) hold:

(1) $P(1)$ is True

(2) $P(k+1)$ is True whenever $P(k)$ is true : $\forall k \in \mathbb{N}$

Proof of equation 2.3 (page 8)

Use the axiom of induction to prove the *Future Value* of an asset is given by equation 2.3. We want to prove that

$$FV_k = FV_0(1+r)^k \quad : \forall k \in \mathbb{N} \qquad \text{eq 2.3}$$

Appendix (optional)

Solution:

First, we note that by definition

$$FV_k = FV_{k-1}(1+r) \qquad \text{eq 2.2}$$

We need to show it works for $n = 1$, which it does.

$$FV_1 = FV_0(1+r)^1$$

Now by the inductive assumption we assume that FV_k is true for an arbitrary natural number $\forall k \in \mathbb{N}$.

$$FV_k = FV_0(1+r)^k \qquad \text{by Assumption}$$

Now test for the $k + 1$ case by applying equation eq 2.2

$$FV_{k+1} = FV_k(1+r)$$
$$= FV_0(1+r)^k (1+r) = FV_0(1+r)^{k+1} \qquad \text{apply eq 2.2}$$

The last equality shows that given FV_k is true for an arbitrary positive natural number k than FV_{k+1} is also true.

We have shown that FV_1, FV_k and FV_{k+1}. Therefore, by the Axiom of Induction FV_n works for ALL, natural numbers (i.e., $\forall n \in \mathbb{N}$) Q.E.D

9 Bibliography

Anderson, J., & Bell, J. (1997). *Number Theory with Applications.* Prentice- Hall Inc.

Mayes, T. R., & Shank, T. M. (2001). *Financial Analysis with Microsoft Excel.* Harcourt Inc.

Pratt, S. P. (1998). *Cost of Capital: Estimation and Applications.* John Wiley & Sons Inc.

www.ingramcontent.com/pod-product-compliance
Lightning Source LLC
Chambersburg PA
CBHW031551210526
45464CB00003B/1259